Straight From My Heart

Diane Wilson

wichmann & co
Music. Message. Legacy.

Publisher: Wichmann & Co, LLC
United States
www.WichmannAndCo.com
hello@wichmannandco.com

ISBN (paperback): 979-8-9934623-2-5
ISBN (ebook): 979-8-9934623-3-2
First Edition, 2025
Printed in the United States of America

This collection contains original poetry written by the author. Any references to people, places, or events reflect the author's personal experiences and creative expression.

Contents

Dedication

This book is dedicated to our son, Jake Charles Wilson.

We only had the one son and in our eyes he was perfect. God blessed us with such a loving and caring son. When you go through life and have the luxury of meeting someone who inspires you to be better - do it!

God sends people to us to help us be our best. I do believe that Jake was that type of person and I thank God for his gifts and for his desire to share them with others. Please take the time to allow others to feel the love you hold for them. Their well being should be our greatest concern. We can bless others with simple words and acts of kindness. We are blessed with beautiful memories of Jake's life filled with love. I'm forever changed; but I'm finding peace thru God's love. Please enjoy your life and appreciate all the many blessings each day brings.

Diane Wilson
November 1, 2025

Texas Roots

A Note From The Author

Howdy ~

I was born in Muskogee, Oklahoma, but I've developed Texas roots. I'm just a country, girl, comfy in my jeans and boots. Poems are a great release for me and some practically write themselves so easily. I hope you will enjoy what I wrote. My thoughts are often scribbled on a note.

I have 2 HEAVENLY ANGELS up above watching over me and sending love too. Thank you for taking your time to read STRAIGHT FROM MY HEART I pray it is the encouragement you need.

Letter From A Friend

For my friend Diane Wilson; In honor of her only son Jake Wilson.

Diane and I have been friends for almost 50 years and throughout this time I have come to love and respect her sweet spirit and God given talent as a prolific Poet. She has always amazed me with a phone call asking me what I thought about a poem she had written in the middle of the night. As she shared her words and heart with me, it is always as though she sees into other hearts and feels their pain or joy. One time I asked how long it took to write one of her moving poems. Her answer was; "About 15 minutes". I said how is that possible? Her answer was; "I don't know. The words just starts to come to me and I grab a paper so i can get them down. Sometimes they come so fast that I just keep grabbing paper to get it all down." I truly believe that God speaks through Diane's prayers and her heart and compassion for others.

Jake was such a Godly young man, Husband, Father and Friend who helped so many people in his 34 years just as Diane does in her life. A mother's love is as no other love and when God took Jake home, she was crushed. Through much prayer she has been given so many beautiful words of comfort and love to be shared with her grandchildren and others.

Diane's book, STRAIGHT FROM MY HEART, started out to be a Christmas gift to her grandchildren and has now become a story of a Mother's forever love. How blessed we are.

Thank you for being my dear friend and allowing me to be a part of sharing your Beautiful Gift. I am blessed to do so for such a kind and compassionate Christian Friend, Mother, Wife and Grandmother.

Vicky L. Gillispie

+/Once upon a time
there was a old woman
Lived in the word Love!

Look Out World

November 11, 2025

That's the sentence Charley Wilson was known to say

He would warn the universe that he was on his way

Charley was well known and respected on all the job sites

He would be the first one there in the morning and the last one to leave at night

I called him good time Charley cause he did love to have fun. Charley got along with everyone.

He loved to cook briskets or steaks for his friends

when you were with Charley the fun would never end.

He was an avid fisherman, and he would go to the rattlesnake roundup each year.

No matter what the task Charley approached it with no fear

When he would go out the front door, he'd say look out world and away he went

Most people heard him say that and they knew what he meant

Charley and I have been together since 1976 and we've had lots of good times

We both loved Willie and went to his picnics to see him and to unwind.

Look out world is so fitting and we've had good laughs with Charley about this

Charley had parties that you wouldn't want to miss

Charley was larger than life and he really loved to have a good time

Charley wore starched jeans and shirt and his boots really shined

He belted out, look out world and gave a fair warning that he was on his way

Charley was very handsome and had a magnetic personality too.

Charley loved life and he would always tell you that he loved you.

He was genuine and such a kind soul

Charley was loved more than he could ever know.

In June, Charley was called to his heavenly home.

He had been in much pain for so long

He was such a strong resilient man
We all thought he would always be here.
Charley is now my Angel and his spirit is still near.
LOOK OUT WORLD!

Harmony

August 29, 2012

Well I have been called Pocahontas...
Yes, the peacemaker of all times
And that has been my hearts desire or dream
For us to live in harmony, laugh, love, and be kind!
From birth, we were taught that kindness begins at home.
With God's help we can do this
For time will continue on
And there are many things we have missed.
Today is what we can work with and change
Please gain strength by calling on "His Name".
Let go and allow God to just come inside
It's thru His love that true harmony abides!
Harmony, harmony it is the Heavenly way
To serve Jesus with those we meet each day
Harmony, harmony will forever be my prayer!
Jesus open our eyes - help us to love and to share
To smile and speak kind words so your kingdom will grow...
As we shine and radiate the peace of God within our soul!

"Finally Brothers and Sisters, farewell, put things in order, listen to my appeal, agree with one another, live in peace; and the God of love and peace be with you."

2 Corinthian 13:11

Be Careful

October 9, 2013

Be careful who you push away
They may be all you have one day!
For life is short - and problems will arise
God places our helpers by our side
So be Careful and accept help when it is given
Then thank God - and get busy living!!!

This Life

April 4, 2017

There have been many times when I've felt as tho I had nothing to give.

As I've aged - I've learned - It's really more about how I lived.

So many mistakes were made along the way,

Broken hearts and friendships and no real appreciation of each day.

It seemed as tho I'd always have another time to fix what went wrong or more time to make it right,

So I'd go to bed mad - always felt the need to hold a grudge or to pick a new fight.

All those times when I felt I had nothing to give I still managed to smile,

Years later - I see that was my gift all the while!

Someone can have talent galore and money to burn

But without a smile - there's no joy in a cent that they earn.

People do matter and we have relationships with them based on the effort we give.

We can take them for granted daily or we can be more aware of the life that they live.

24 hours are available to everyone daily and in each minute we have a choice...

We can think compliments and relay them with our voice.

I urge you to love - really love your family and friends.

Be mindful at any moment it can come to an end.

It is a given that love hurts and it is not easy to go thru everyday

But we can change our attitude and watch what we say.

I've been the one to lash out and try to get even with those that did me wrong...
But the joy that produced - never lasted long.
So please pause as you go about every single minute
And remember to be present in it!

I do wish this love for life would have came to me during the hard times I went thru
Instead, I was lost and just didn't know what to do.
Hurt and then hurt back was my only theme
Nothing genuine and no one cared or so it seemed.

Much later in life, around 40 to be exact...
I discovered that God forgave me and that He has my back!!
It did make decisions and my actions weren't ones I was proud of
But I learned to react is not the way to show my love...

I wasn't supposed to act at all - I only needed to be the real me.
God made me and that is who others see...
Not the flawed person who tried and failed and just couldn't win...
But I became the person who is forgiven of my sins!!

I really hope I can reach anyone who may be hurting like I did
If so, please know our God forgives.
Don't wait and think I will make it right one day...
It just might not work out that way.

Love will always conquer and help you win
Live - just live - this life you are in!!

The Best Way Is God's Way

October 21, 2016

When I say I'm done - I don't mean you any harm

That's just the fact - I'm focused on God, my family, and farm

God has a way of helping us to sort out and remember what matters most to me...

That's why I'm listening to Him and trying harder just to be.

The person He wanted - resulting in a better follower and better wife

He says we should love everyone and Lord knows I do try!

His commandments are to be honored and we are not to ask why.

His way are higher than ours and we simply can't understand

So we tend to find fault and often refuse when others lend a helping hand.

One thing I have learned is it is not about me...

That has helped when hurt and anger won't let me be,

People are at different levels on their Christian walk.

They may not even realize how rudely they talk.

It doesn't matter how much a person tries to offend

What matters most is that they have God as their true friend.

He knows our heart and if we give Him the pieces

He can mend it and see that such nonsense ceases.

God has much better things for us to do

It is a good life He has promised and planned for me and for you!

I'm thankful for my new way of thinking and of my new insight...

My future needs only God's love and His light.

Many days and hours are now spent

Reading His words and remembering to repent.

We are human and we will surely fail

He wants us to get strong and quit being frail.

Our bodies and minds are an awesome gift we should preserve...

It would be the best way and will help us to serve.

We not only allow others to witness what a blessing we have become to all

We also can be better warriors for His kingdom and we surely won't fall.

The things I'm "done with" are trying to make wrongs right

I've given it all to God and now I sleep better at night.

Fear and hurt are the devil's way of creeping in...

I refuse to allow any more of such sin.

So God's way are the best

And in His loving arms - I find my rest!

The Change

April 20, 2017

There is so much that I will never understand
Like how a life can be taken by a family member's hand
I know accidents can happen and they often do
But there are also times when someone plans to harm you!

In life we don't like to think or talk about these dark events
However, the truth is - revenge and hate is how some life's are spent!
It is so sad that a life can be taken in a blink of an eye...
It's never up to us how anyone should die!

Instead of thoughts to cut short someone's chance to live;
How about using that talent and resources to give
It would be great to think that we all felt the same...
To appreciate each day, be loving and stop playing games!

These are thoughts that I can't seem to make sense of
Why anyone would hate and never give love?
They say that criminals have a brilliant mind...
Often they weren't shown compassion,
nor did they experience a relationship of any kind.

I guess I will never be able to change anyone's heart but mine...
But I will always be hoping that as I go thru life, I may find
Others that share a love for life and find value in our every heartbeat...
People think of others and have thoughts that are sweet.

Maybe I'm a dreamer - but that's OK by me...
For I truly dislike all the horror I see.
When no pure thought is given
And there is no love for living!

Yes that's a reality for some that behave this way -
They spew hate and intend to harm with words that they say!
I will only be held accountable for what I say and do...
Please recognize the change we need begins with me and you!

Each day we can make the difference we want to see -
One kind word or smile might just set someone free!
What a joy to know that simple jester could change someone's heart
Be that change - being good and doing your part!!

God's On A Roll Again

May 22, 2017

God is on a roll again...
And He is even better than the coolest friend.
He forgave my sins and He saved my soul -
And in my life He is in complete control.

Sometimes what God does is very small
Sometimes you wonder if He is there at all.
But lately it is so plain to see...
That God has done so much for me!

God is on a roll again
He knows just when we need a friend.
He brings warmth and beauty that we need
His love sprouts in us like garden seeds.

We are so blessed to have His love
It is so very nice to always be thought of!
Even in the early morning dew
Our God is watching out for you.

Sometimes it's simple -
Like the perfectly timed call on the phone...
An added assurance -
We are not alone!

God's on a roll again
And He proves it daily by being our friend.
I love how God can do so much
And I am thrilled to be able to feel His touch!

My heart is full and the joy that God gives is real
Try to be still and His love you will feel.
God does so many things; it is important for us to stop and relax -
We don't have to stay on guard - He has our back!!

God can help with anything we may be going thru
It is important to remember He knows all and He will help you!
So give thanks and show your appreciation in every way -
God will be very pleased with the words you say!

God is on a roll again
Get with his momentum and roll thru life's curve and bends!
When God is on a roll again
You will know how beautiful our days can be...from beginning to end!!!

Lord

September 4, 2016

Lord I ask you to come into my heart
I have no room for bitterness, unforgiving, or fear.
I ask your help to mend relationships that have fallen apart
And to rekindle the love of our family we hold so dear.

There can be no true meaning without you to guide
Please come into my heart and walk by my side
Help me to see the good in all i meet
And help me to be your hands and feet.

I love you Lord and I want to walk in Your light
I have faith that your ways are always right.
Lord, I ask you to come into my heart
Turn this sinner - Lord - into a work of art.

Your plans are perfect and your plans are in place...
Help me Lord as I finish my race.
I'm sorry that I tried to do things on my own...
I see my mistakes and how I've grown.

Lord I ask you to come into my heart
Be with me Lord as each day starts!
Show me how to live a life that will honor you
Help me to apply your words in all I do

I love you Lord but on this Earth I sometimes feel so alone
I will continue to praise your name till you call me home.
Please give me words to help others to see
This hope of a brighter future you have placed in me!

Life's Relationships

We go through life with an attitude about different ones we meet
We act as tho we are the ones on the judgement seat.
It is as if we don't care about him or about her
And it isn't till much time goes by does our heart seem to stir...
Then we remember it wasn't about her or him
It has always been about God and them
When we become thankful for the ones we are blessed to see -
That builds a better relationship between God and me!

This Thing Called Life

July 22, 2016

We are all on different roads

And what we pass has true meaning I am told

God's plan was all about love -

Just know the people we meet are sent from above!

Don't grow weary and tired and turn a blind eye

To the many people and things as you pass by.

There is a reason why your journey is this way

And it makes a difference what we think and what we say.

Don't make a blanket statement of your own view

But be open and suggest other things to do.

Our way is important - but only to us...

Try to see the whole picture and avoid any fuss!

This thing called life IS God's great plan.

He has laid a blueprint for every woman and man.

So try hard to see the good in each day

And please remember the importance of the words we say.

People are hurting and there are things that we can do

If you want a difference - it begins with you!!

This thing called life is a true blessing indeed

Don't walk it alone - find others and fill their needs!

Forgive Me Lord

August 28, 2017

Forgive me Lord when I think my life is so bad
I take no account of what I've got and long for what I had.
I know your plans are working out just like you have planned
I just get mixed up and my emotions get out of hand.

Forgive me Lord if I ever seem to take your love for granted
I know you know best and often my views are slanted
I try to think of why and what instead of letting it be
I should know not to doubt because you are always there for me!

Forgive me Lord when I don't give thanks for all that you do
I may even take credit for gifts that were given by you!
You are the one constant in these ever changing days!
Forgive me Lord if what I do doesn't line up with what I say.

I've grown so much and I know that you are the reason why
Forgive me Lord and help me when I can't do anything but cry!
I love you Lord and I really do know how very good you are
Forgive me Lord when I know these things and still worship you from afar.

It is my hearts desire to be more pleasing to you
Forgive me Lord if I need daily reminders too.
I'm sorry Lord that I fail to express my endless love
As there are no words for the beauty you provide in the Heavens up above!

I'll try again to be patient Lord, and if I slip you will be there
For your love is amazing and nothing on Earth can compare!
Forgive me Lord just one more time and I'll be sure to get it right
I thank you for watching over me all my days and my nights.

I trust you and I know you are everything I need
Forgive me Lord and I will continue to praise all your good deeds.
There is no other reason to continue my walk without you.
I promise Lord, I'll walk a better path and always look up to you!

Forgive me Lord for the times I've strayed and gotten off the path
I made mistakes and I can't count them all - I'm just not that good at math.
Forgive me Lord for looking at all things in such a wrong way
Help me Lord - I want you always near me each and every day!

Your ways are higher than mine - this is true
And with your help Lord - Peace and love will be what I give and what I do!!

Texting With Jesus

I got a text from Jesus - It was a gentle reminder to me
To further his kingdom and share His love with all I see
He has so much to do that is why he counts on me and you!

His message was to care about everyone each day...
We can help uplift them with the kind words that we say
Please do your part in helping our Father up above...

His "LOL" means Love Only Love!!!

If I Only Had Today

July 13, 2017

If I only had today
There would be so much I'd want to say
Or would I choose actions instead?
There would be so much going thru my my head.

On any given day - someone hurts us or gets in our way...
Would I focus on that, or would I just go play?
God would be the main one I should be talking to
For He alone could guide me as to what to do.

It would be sad to know I only had one day
To hug, love, cry, pray and fumble for the words to say
I'd want my loved ones to know how very much I care
And I'd try to think of photos and other moments to share.

For after a loved one does pass
Those are the things that we grasp.
We always think we have lots of time
And if that's true - things could work out just fine.

But if I only had today
I'd need to make amends - come what may!
I wouldn't want to leave this world with any regrets
And I couldn't bear to have any unforgiveness or obligations I've not met.

We tend to avoid the subject and pretend it won't happen at all

But if it did - I'm sure whose name we would call

So call on your Savior - you'll know what to say

Start that conversation now - as if you only had today!

A God Centered Life

October 28, 2013

Why do we have to live our life
Before we want to share it
We have opportunity or strife
As we find our way - see where we fit

But if we had confidence and kept our cool
We could have learned many things, not taught in school
For instance, Mom and Dad were always close by
My thoughts were its my life - let me try!

Did not take time to ask or reason
I'd show up once or twice depending on the season.
Do you see this pattern happening to you
If so, change it - take control of you.

Realize we mean the world to our family and friends
And we've been blessed with special relationships that never end.
We shouldn't try to live our lives before we share it
Instead, let this time we have to remind us to not quit!

We need to be there and be involved each day
Really be concerned about what others think and say.
After all is said and done
You will see the joy that you bring to everyone.

Life is hard if we don't use our gifts to help others
No better place to start than with our Father and our Mother.
There is no way to repay the love they give
They want you to be comfortable where you live.

Grab this blessing we call our Mom and Dad
Live out your life enjoying every good memory and forgive any bad!
Be on purpose about living an awesome God loving life on Earth...
And don't ever forget who loved you since birth

Dare to share and grow with loved ones - don't grow apart
Experiences are blessings - begin everyday with an open heart.
God will work out each and every small detail
Put God first in life and you will never fail!

Offering

June 25, 2017

There was a time in my life
I dreamed of only being a Mom, a Wife...
But since I've aged and spiritually grew,
My thoughts are more of what Jesus does - for you!

Now I prepare each week for my offering or tithe
And I give my Lord, my Father, my life!
With this new dream or desire in me -
I'm more concerned about giving constantly
And I'd rather help someone - than to focus on me!

My relationship with God is how I have grown
This comfort and joy began with mere seeds being sown.
The best advice I now will give
Is to choose for whom you want to live.
And God willing, you will see the light too
Then watch as God works wonders for you!

Pray each day and give of yourself...
Your offering isn't always measured by wealth.
It is the way we talk and the things we say
That can shine a light and help pave the way!

Yes, a seed planted and a light that shines -
A plan hopefully for you - but it's definitely mine!

Love All People

April 1, 2020

Love all people... sounds easy, right?
It is easy to love the loveable and to hug them tight!

But, then out of nowhere this Coronavirus came to disrupt our land...
It has demanded attention and quickly took the upper hand.

With this silent threat - nothing is the same.
One by one the daily events that we knew were cancelled and changed.

The theaters, bowling, and all types of entertainment came to a stop.
Jobs have been lost, routines changed, causing a huge strain on big companies and on the
    Mom and Pop.

People will hoard things and sometimes show a selfish side
This can also be a time of honesty and bravery and hope shared worldwide.

Love all people; please do it today...
Don't pick and choose who to help and who to turn away.

There is a lack of compassion and many material necessities that people can't find.
The empty shelves tend to weigh heavy on our minds.

The devil would love for you to give up hope in these trying times.
But remember, God knows the ending and we will be just fine.

Use this time to take care of yourself and hold your loved ones near.
God is on the throne and His love will cast out all fear.

Love all people; please do it today...
Make loving others be what we do and what we say.

There is hope of all things working together for good to them that love God so be of good
    cheer.
Praise God and with prayer we will unite and conquer our fears.

During our shelter in place we are following a 6 foot rule to claim our space.
This deadly virus knows no gender, age, or race.

So fear will not be what others see
I'm strong and I have the love of God in me!

Together our strengths will be multiplied.
Let's be the light and let God be our guide.

Love all people; please do it today...
Make loving others be what we do and what we say!

Living A Yes Lord Life

August 22, 2023

I am living a yes Lord life

Striving to be a better friend, and a better wife

Making a conscious decision to improve more each day

And helping others along my way.

By saying Yes Lord I aim to please

I seek His guidance on bended knees

Yes Lord every morning and all the day thru

Yes Lord I will follow you

Your commandments are to be kept and never broken

The Bible has red letters for the words the Lord has spoken;.

Yes Lord in the morning and Yes lord before I sleep at night

Saying Yes Lord will start my day off right

Living a Yes Lord life will forever be

The path the Lord wants for me.

He has provided the Bible, so find time to read

The scriptures can bring hope and plant a seed

God's promises are true take heed

He will provide strength in our time of need

Living a Yes Lord life and sharing His word each day

Spreading love with the kind words we say.

Yes Lord I want to really know you

Show me what you want me to do

Living a Yes Lord life by helping everyone you meet each day

Always say Yes Lord, and He will pave the way

***

*Inspired by story about the words... YES LORD embroidered and framed hung at the foot
of her Mom's bed.*
Each day and night these two words were always said.
Some may think your legacy must be about silver or gold
But the Bible is the richest story ever told
As we say Yes Lord and put our trust in Him to let him be our guide
We show our faith in Him as we travel far and wide.
To put a thought, or share a story of God's love
Is a blessing sent from up above.
Say Yes Lord and always do your best
Grow your faith in The Lord and you will find rest.

Life

Can you really see me from afar?

How observant you are!

Maybe you should look a little closer to see

Those things aren't all that bad about me.

I don't drink and forget where to stop

I've changed my life - and I have more respect for the cops.

No pill or any amount of smoke

Would do anything but keep me broke!

I also know it can't compare to what's in store

As we strive to get to Heaven's shores.

Seriously, instead of pointing out my flaws...

This gentle reminder should give you pause.

We all have stuff we rather not have told

A friend and confident is worth more than gold!

We are more alike than we differ - this I know

And we can give others a hand no matter where we go.

Life is short and it is best when we get busy living each day

Our words are so important so watch what you say!

We think we know what others think and feel

Without speaking with them - that's not a good deal!

God has great plans for our life and for our loved ones too

Make sure you Honor God in all you do!

The Greatest Love Of All

January 2, 2020

One person steps in
And one steps out
It's complicated but
I'll explain what I'm talking about
In life it seems as though
One gets to come in
And one has to go
Just like that one will lose and one will win
Many times we are the winner and yet we don't see
We sit and complain and think poor me
Best thing any of us can do is to pray
Ask God where we should go and what we should say
It seems as if our life is perfect but then it falls apart
But does it really and when did this trouble start
We can't go through life taking for granted all that comes our way
We really should love others and push any bad thoughts away
If we honor God and try our best
We can be more peaceful and we will find rest.
God is near each and every day
He waits for us to call on Him and say
We are sorry for our sins
And when, as we confess we invite Him in.
Try to worry less about what others do
Keep your focus on how to be a better you
It's not our place to say who comes and goes

God has that planned out and only He knows

When things are rough and we don't understand

God is right there waiting for us to ask His plan

Please don't waste your life worrying about what others do or what they say

Just know God can make a way

My prayer for you my friend

Is that you walk with God and confess your sins

Before it's too late I hope we all can see

The problems we're pointing out in others keep us from being free.

Let go let God and just let things be

If you're truly bothered and no one seems to care

Remember God loves you so take your concerns to Him in prayer

Don't sit on the sideline of life and let it pass you by

What joy and peace you'll find if you really try

No we can't do everything alone and God is just waiting for us to call

Invite him into your heart and you will know the greatest love of all.

What Matters To Me

November 26, 2019

We go thru life and we stumble and fall
As we try and try to make sense of it all.
It's too bad that we are much older when we finally see
That peace and love are what matters to me!
When we are young, we are full of doubt
We think we are the only ones to care about
We never take time to check on others who live alone...
We don't stop by or even pick up the phone.
Too much is taken for granted, and then it is gone
When was your last conversation - has it really been that long?
We say that we trust in God and He knows the way
But when we get off His path we find that is a big price to pay
It's never smooth sailing when you ignore all the signs
God sends us signals but obey is not on our mind.
What matters to me is to live and let be
But God tells us to love all those in need
We could share our testimony and plant that seed
There has to be more to life than all the struggles we see
I want others to find value in what matters to me!
God gave us a heart to care for people and to give them a lift
Simple things show love and remind us... life is a true gift!
Thankful, grateful, and blessed you see
This is my life song and it is what matters to me!

It's not The Same

April 4, 202

It's not the same since you are not in my life anymore
I still welcome your presence, but you don't darken my door
You may call me by mistake, but I wish it was with intent
The friendship we shared was really Heaven sent.
I thought of you as a sister, and I still have nothing but love for you
I miss our long talks, and lots of laughter too.
Life can throw a curveball, and you'll never see it heading your way
Our friendship is gone and I did not even have a say
In this life people come and some people move away
I just try to remember all the good times we enjoyed along the way
Sometimes things will happen that we don't understand
We need to count our blessings and remember God has a plan
It's not the same Since you are not in my life like you used to be
Your name popping up on my call list was sure good to see
I wish you well. I love you much and I want the best for you
God, please bless my friend and her precious family too
Life is too short to hold a grudge when things happen that we don't understand
Thank you Lord, for the blessing of realizing that with your help, I can
I have a strong faith that all will work out the way it's meant to be
Thank you God for the work you've done in me
I may not see you or talk to you on the phone
You will always be welcome in my home
It's not the same without you here with me
But things work out the way they are meant to be.

Each Day Is A Blessing

January 28, 2020

Each day is a blessing - that's what some say

But if that's the truth

Shouldn't we be in the moment and more aware in every way of the missed opportunities and times that could have been better spent?

We missed those opportunities and the time flew and our relationships went...

To a place of hurt and disgust

To conversations becoming non-existent because people have betrayed your trust.

Being a blessing each day is surely a more positive way

Make this change and a real love will be there to connect with each day

In life our hope comes from above

From our Father in Heaven - who pours out His love.

A love like no other - freely given - ours to embrace

This is accomplished when we seek His face.

Every day is a blessing and these words are true.

It's a proven fact that Jesus is the one who's for you in all you do

So during times when you doubt and times when you feel broken

You can trust in Jesus and all the Promises He has spoken.

You will find peace and value and see a better day...

If you turn to Jesus - He will make a way.

See all the good and you can be a light

With God's help make each day a blessing and all things will be alright.

When You See Me

May 30, 2020

When you see me, what do you see?

Is it even possible that you see the real me?

With our rushed schedules that are so hectic on most days

This creates division and we go our separate ways.

We never really stop and simply unwind...

And so we let things build up between us instead of speaking our mind.

Relationships can be stronger when the effort is given

Our God has blessed us with our friends and family in this life we are living.

They say hurting people hurt people and I believe it's true

I don't doubt it at some point in my life I was hurt and in turn I hurt you.

Good intentions can't mend a relationship or keep it in tack

To really appreciate the people in our lives we need to remember that fact

People often say words and their actions may not reflect the way they really feel.

So we get offended and question if this friendship is real

The devil is all excited when this hurt occurs

No matter to him, if it is a him or a her.

Sometimes whole families are torn apart

They won't work it out - and they've hardened their heart.

The reason for that is simple you see.

Instead of looking for faults when you look at me...

Could we try, at least for a while,

To see the good and even share a smile

Friends and families are to be cherished and loved

They are the true blessings sent from God above.

Follow God's lead and whatever you do

I hope you really see me having no desire to hurt you.

Then when you see me I hope you see

I'm just a child of God trying to live up to the life He has planned for me.

When you see me what do you see?

I'm a sinner that's longing to be set free

The Bible explains that everlasting love and peace in Heaven we will see .

Next time you see me look for the changes that God is making in me.

Say What You Need To Say

May 26. 2021

Not everyone gets to live another day

Please don't live with any regrets

Of others needs you

"Could have" met.

Sometimes a simple hug would mean so much

It brings hope and love with just your touch

We live in a fast paced world and often forget

Are there calls we haven't returned yet

With the best of intentions it still happens every day

We think it's okay because tomorrow I will say what I need to say.

Let's try to simply block out a few minutes of time

This would help build relationships and be a good sign

To remind us how we must work hard each day

To be more present each moment and say what you need to say.

Being genuine is a trait that is very rare

But it all comes down to how much do you care

Make those you love be a priority each and every day.

Communication is so important please say what you need to say

Life is full of twist and turns

It's only with age that we really learn

Our younger self was carefree and not concerned of what to eat or drink

Now we are more aware of our surroundings but remain less vocal about what we think.

We are all just travelers and we hope to find our way

Those we meet have real value so cherish those moments and please always say what you
need to say!

Things aren't what they used to be, doesn't mean they're bad, doesn't mean they're sad
Our lives hold more than our family tree
We have divine appointments and folks placed in our path each day
We could be entertaining Angels so love should be what we do and what we say

Don't get caught up in worldly things and keep yourself sin free
We start off with just the basics in life and wind up wanting everything we see
Which becomes a habit and an enticing lure
Sadly, wanting more and more is pointless and has no cure.

There hope is in God's Promises
of an eternal life for you and me
Trust our loving God and repent to be set free!

Those Are Just Words

I know you are talking and I'm listening to what you say

I don't understand your "vacation day"

I've heard that said a time or two

Having a "vacation day" is nothing I know how to do.

My travels are few and airports are not where I belong.

All my life, I've never planned a trip, short or long

If I earned that time off I took the pay and just stayed till my shift was done

Yes, quite boring, predictable and no fun!!

Words we say can describe and explain how we had a good time

Or words can tell a story from a book and connect your heart and mine

I hear you talking and I would love to relate

Let's find other things to enjoy and to debate.

"Vacation day" has never materialized for me

Those are just words describing a life some never get to see.

Judgement Day

June 9, 2022

Lord help me make a difference and show the way to you
I want my life to matter in every thing I say and do

We have a chance to help others every single day
Lord help me reach them and show them the way

Our life on Earth is like a vapor, here today and gone tomorrow
Lord help me to help others rise above their sorrows.

An eternal life with you is our reward for a life well lived
Please help us to be mindful to take less than we give

Thank you Lord for the beauty you created all around us
Please help us focus on a better life without any fuss

Help me be a light and leave the dark behind
Lord, I want to be a light and to love and be kind.

I'm sad that others go thru life ad never seem to see
That they too can help to set others free

We don't have to quote scripture to show the life you planned
We only need to show compassion to our fellow man

Lord your ways are higher than ours, please let us remember
We must be mindful of broken hearts and we must be tender

We have a chance as we go about our day
To lift up others by just being aware of what we say

We love you Lord, and please help us and hear us pray
We want to be with you, Lord, and receive Your blessing on Judgement Day

The Cross

Take up your cross and follow me
This total surrender will set you free.
The eternal reward is well worth any temporary pain
Following Christ produces our "Heavenly Gain"
In life we all have our cross to bear
Life's ups and downs aren't always fair
To follow Christ doesn't promise we won't have sorrow
For in Him we find our joy and our hope is for tomorrow
Our strength and understanding continues to grow

When we study God's word we become more aware of how God loves us,
So take up your cross and follow me
God can not work miracles if we don't invite Him in
Cherish your friends and families and don't give in to sin
God has a great plan and a purpose for our life too
Allow God to unfold His plan He has offered to you
When we take up our cross and follow this path we will plainly see
God's abundant blessings showered upon you and me

Live each day as tho it is your last
Forgive often and don't dwell on the past
Follow the examples of Jesus and His disciples too
Love everyone and the life that God planned for you!

Heavenly Memories

I have fond memories of how I have grown
And these were made with the seeds that were sown
These Heavenly memories are now mine to tell
I pray my memories might ring a bell...
To alert others that God is the answer, always
And this wisdom is reached as one prays.

Yes, I've gone thru some valleys and had many fears,
I now praise God and I have changed thru the years!
When I remember how I had never thought of Him or His words in my past
My Savior's forgiveness comes to my memory and His guidance I still ask.

How could I have seen all the wonderful things He made
And never think of Him and all the gifts He gave?
When I remember how things were long ago
I'm more thankful for the Lord, I now know!

Heavenly memories, who'll share my memories of things that were meant to be
He's my redeemer and may His light forever shine in me.
My faith was small but thru His word it grew
God's love is forever and my memories now are of my life made anew!
These Heavenly memories of the life He planned for me...
Is such an abundantly peaceful place to be!!

Heavenly memories, Heavenly memories are now mine to tell
Yes, all the good news about how I've been blessed so well
The new purpose and new power that I start with each day -
Are how God has helped me to know what to say.
God's love is forever and His promises are true
Please accept Him into your life and enjoy all He will do for you!

I Look To The Sky

I look to the sky and study the clouds
I want to see you and say hi and I want you to know that you make me proud.
Your mind, your voice, your heart are greatly missed
I could go on - I've got quite a list!

I know God took you because your work here is done
But that doesn't help those left here - we miss you a ton!
I do look to the sky
And most times I just wonder why
I try to trust Jesus and such
But Son - I miss you so much!

You got things out of order is what I think in my mind
My world since you left has started to unwind.
There was so much that I still wanted to say
And I just keep talking to you every day

Your smile is etched in my mind for sure -
And till I see you again, God's promises will be my cure
My heart is broken and I look for you in everything I see
God knows - you mean so much to me!

I always knew you were special and you always gave my spirits a lift
What a joy from God - our Son - our gift!
Till God calls me home
I won't feel alone.

You are in my heart
Just like from the start!
Your friends and beautiful children can help us get by
Especially on those days when I ask God why.

God had his reasons and I know you are in His loving arms
In Heaven - I'm sure all is beautiful and all are free from any harm.
Why we think this world is so great and we don't want to leave
If we just know God has great plans for us up His sleeve.

I look to the sky and I study the clouds
I want to hear you sing and turn it up loud
Till we can walk those streets of gold together - I'll keep your precious memory alive.
And I will thank God for the years He allowed you to be by my side.

I love you son -
And yes, your work here is done.
We all miss your laughter and the joy you brought into the room
You are so special and yes you left us way too soon!

We trust in the Lord and His grace we will wait
Till that day we meet at Heaven's gate!
Till then I will study the clouds and try hard to see
Your big smile looking down at me!

Another Angel Just Got Wings

August 30, 2025

Another angel just got wings
If it's our friend or family, we don't like to think of these things
Many loved ones and beloved friends have gone to Heaven above
With them, they take a piece of our heart and all of our love
God knows everything and He knows the number of our days
We just need to continue to share God's love with everyone we meet and pray
It's not by chance when we talk to people on the street
They are put in our path through God's divine plan
He provides and we need to invest all that we can
We get sad when our loved ones are gone to their forever home
We don't think of their happiness we just think of being alone
What a joy they must feel they are in Heaven
And they know it's real

Another angel just got wings
Think about the true happiness that this brings
They won't have the trials or sorrow that we experience here on earth each day
True joy and beauty and eternal happiness pave their way
We tend to think of how sad we are without our loved ones near
God wants us to realize the words of the Bible are not just pleasant to hear
God has designed everything and He has so much to give
A mansion on a hilltop
Will be where we live

Choosing to follow Jesus is how we will experience this joy, God is waiting for us to repent
and share the world with every girl and boy
Another angel just got wings
Live your best life and be mindful of what eternity brings

Slipping Away

October 30, 2025

Slipping away when we were younger was a treat and a fun time

We enjoyed ourselves and now those memories replay in our mind

This slipping away is a part of life and is sad to see

Yesterday you remembered who i was but today you don't know me

I guess the main thing we can do is to help each other age and try to stay well

We are all on this journey and we all have a story to tell

When we are little we don't understand how we have our whole life to live

We take for granted that we will always have more to give

God only knows why our memories fade and we start to forget

We can't remember our loved ones and all the friends we have met.

Thank you God for the joy we have known

Help us to understand and to remember things we are shown

We age and we become childe-like and innocent again

Protect us God and bless us with some good friends

The road we travel might become unfamiliar or hard to endure

But God is with us and on that we can always be sure

So as we live and we love those we meet each day

Protect our minds God from slipping away

Will Do

August 20, 2017

The last words I texted to you
Were for you to rest well tonight - you said 'will do'.
I won't forget how hard it was to watch you go
Jake, my Son, the love I have for you - some may never know.
It isn't that since you are gone - I love you more
I simply can't put into words all that you stood for.
I take comfort from talking with your wide array of friends...
It's amazing how that love grows - and never ends.
Son, your life was so short and now my heart is broke,
I cling to our photos and memories of the last time we spoke.
My life now has found a new purpose and drive
I have to stay busy by keeping all of your memories alive.
Your children are asking at what age you started to sing so well
Jake, your shoes are hard to fill and there is so much I want to tell.
Thank you for being the man we remained so proud of
Thanks as well for daily showering so many with your love
I'm so very thankful that the Lord gave us you
I know loving and honoring you forever is what I will do
The work ethic you developed and perfected is always in demand.
Your legacy will be that of a well respected man
Jake, I've been your cheerleader even before you were born
That is why my heart is crushed, battered and torn.
The mere thought of my days without you
Makes it exceptionally hard to move forward but move forward - I will do.
I want you to return and then I think what that would mean

I've learned so much and God has revealed things aren't what they seem.

Yes, you are in Heaven and I really long to be there with you.

Till God calls me home - Son loving you will be the most perfect thing I always will do!!

Gone But Not Forgotten

July 31, 2018

You are missed morning, night and noon
I keep wishing to get your call or text soon

You would prefer my mood to be up instead of down
I can't help it - I'm still looking for you to pull into town.

Comfort comes when your life song and your walk with God is known
Your relationship with God has deepened and grown

You sang and shared about this true love while you lived
This message is eternal and no greater gift could you give

Your presence was a present - which I plainly see
Thankful for the memories of your giving and loving so free

I'm strengthened with each mention of your name
There are multiple changes - nothing is the same

The best thing that I find comfort in
We all know God promises death is not the end.

The love of a Mother and Son is forever, so loving you is what I'll do
Each memory is cherished and I'm eternally thankful for you.

The work you put into each relationship was so real
It's that love that is helping us to heal

You are walking with God and "HE" has you in a much better place
On Earth we just miss you, your voice and handsome face.

The message you shared thru song and even your tattoos
Will forever be sweet memories of you!

Without You

November 26, 2017

Made it thru September and October

My heart is broken - but I'm still sober

This is the last week of November already

The pain I feel remains steady.

I realized today that this is the longest we've ever been apart.

That magnifies my pain and hurts my heart

This is a different kind of pain

I'm not moving forward - no I'm the same

The day you went to your Heavenly Home

My world was shattered and I feel so alone.

Without you

What am I to do

You would want me to live

To reach out to others and to give

Whether it be money or my time

Sharing the love of God - letting my light shine.

I go thru the motion in most things that I do

Life seems so empty without you

I love you and I promise your name lives on

I'm sharing your favorite scriptures and playing your songs

Your voice has gone silent on the earthly realm

But in Heaven's choir - you may be at the helm

God called you for an important job to do

We weren't ready for you to go - but HE needed you

Without you

So much to do
Your shoes are hard to fill
We miss you like crazy - and we always will!
God's promises are what helps us each day
With God we are shown the way
He has us all in the palm of His hand
Help us Lord and heal our land.

Would You Facetime Me Jesus

December 2, 2017

Would you FaceTime me Jesus... I know you know why
My Son Jake is with you now - yet all I do is cry!
It occurred to me that a quick FaceTime just might do the trick
I'm not processing this well - I'm making myself sick.
My handsome son came to you just three months ago
He IS with you Jesus, that is our belief and most assuring to know.
But even tho Heaven has so much to offer my Son;
I'm still trying to grasp that his time on Earth is done
I'd love to hug his neck and see all the trophies he has won.
He had such a plan thought out and really had just begun.
He served you well Jesus and shared his faith till the very end
You know that Jesus - you and Jake are great friends.

Would you FaceTime me Jesus? I've tried to explain why
Can we test my connection and just give it a try?
I miss Jakes' smile, his voice, and to see and hear him is what I long for
It is so hard to think I won't hear him sing anymore.
Jesus, please consider and I will appreciate anything I can get
I'm praying and wanting to find peace in it.
A quick glance of Jake's Heavenly home
Would be a glimpse of glory and reminder he is not alone.
He is with you Jesus, and for that we truly give you praise.
This Mama wants to say a special thanks for this awesome Son you helped me raise!
I love you Jesus; and I mean no disrespect by bringing my request to you.
I'm constantly curious about his Heavenly Home and what he is up to.

If FaceTime isn't an option - will you please tell Jake that I love him,
that each day I will try
To have more faith and completely trust Jesus,
and let His word be what I continue to live by.
Please give Jake a hug for me, I have so many beautiful memories,
I'll cherish each and every one.
Thank you Jesus for your Promises of an eternal life with you
I will dive deeper into Your word and continue to trust you too
Everything is in Your timing so with faith i can grow my trust
What an unconditional love you give freely to all of us.
Jesus I feel better and I know in you I gain more strength
I know life is about quality, not about length
Thank you again for all the blessings and love you give
My Son led by example and showed even Mom how to truly LIVE!

Hurting

September 10, 2017

I know I'm hurting and that you are hurting too
For I was his Mom but he means the world to you!
My heart is breaking and yet beating at the same time
How can I be without this precious Son of mine?

I see you and acknowledge that you are in pain
This love we both had makes our loss the same
God only knows why we had to say goodbye
I'm trying to move forward but all I do is cry!

It's clear that we are broken and our normal is gone without a trace
I can't understand him being gone and I'm left longing to see his face.
Jake was a believer and a dreamer, and he never slowed down
How I miss his laughter - he was so much fun to be around.

There is no right or wrong way to just deal
God will see us thru this and He will help us heal
Give your loved ones a hug, and really show them that you care
Let them know that you want them to come to see you and to just be there

Time goes by too fast and in an instant all we know can change
Then you'll be left with just memories and nothing will be the same!
Jake would want us to be happy and to continue to live
He knew all too well it's not about what you have but about what you give.

Oh, I love you Son and miss you more each day
God please help give me peace is how I now will pray!!
I love you Son and your handsome face and your special smile
I know you were never mine - but God just shared you for awhile.

You left a beautiful legacy in your short 34 years
You were so much to so many that's why we cry these tears
Your children will know how much you did on this Earth.
I'm so thankful that you loved them and raised them right from birth!

God has you now in the palm of His hand
And it is much clearer to me about those grains of sand.
Yes, I'm hurting and others are hurting too
All too soon you left us Son - and now it's your work in Heaven to do!

Our prayers will remain for your family and God will help us in all we do
It is just so hard to go on each day without you
In God's promises will be our hope and also in those healing hands of time
I'm so thankful for your life - you awesome Son of mine

Heaven

October 8, 2025

I don't want to just see Heaven... I want to be there for eternity with you

I want to live an everlasting life of love and praise to the King of Glory who makes all
  things new

Thank you Lord for the blessings and love written in the good book

You paid for our sins, what a sacrifice that took

Reading your word helps us to stay on the right path

Sharing scripture can rescue a soul and provide a life raft.

Oh, Lord. Help us to stay focused on all that you provide

Life will be beautiful if you are our guide.

Lord, keep me off the path that is wide

Teach me to walk on the narrow road with you by my side.

I don't want to just see Heaven... I want to be there with you

Come in to my heart and show me what to do

Your kingdom is what is most important, always

Help me honor you and spread love all of my days.

He's Got You

September 19, 2021

Jake, you are in Heaven and we sure miss you

That is a mixed blessing that is hard to get used to!

God said He will be with us always

Since you left Jake, there have been real hard days.

We have photos, CDs, and notes you wrote.

The most cherished memory of all is your bass boat.

So many plans and dreams that show your life was well lived.

The best realization is how freely and cheerfully you would give.

Jake, we miss you and we think of you in all we do.

We are trying to live knowing that God has got you.

God saw how much life you lived out each day.

You pointed others to God after you learned that God is the light and the way.

Your voice so beautifully would sing God's praises.

Our best accomplishment in life is the God loving son we raised.

He's got you and God's plan will be revealed in time.

God can make everything turn out fine.

There is a comfort in knowing you are in God's hands.

We thank Him for the joy you brought as you traveled this land.

Jake, you gave water to those who needed it

You walked by faith and on the praise team your skills did fit.

We know we were blessed to have such an awesome Son.

Thank you God for our healing has begun

Heaven knows our hearts and that we want to be with you

So thankful that loving God was so easy for you to do.

We felt His presence when you sang praise to God so sweet.

We thanked God on bended knee for your voice and your hands and feet

He's got you Jake and we do miss you so much Son

We're leaning on God 's Promises and we always thank God for the race you won.

He's got you and all the Angels rejoices

Heaven must be magnificent when Angels lift their voices!

Our time left here on Earth will be a reminder that we are not done.

We need to be a witness, share scriptures, and shine like our Son.

As we have aged, we learned that God has a plan for our lives.

It doesn't matter if it is Sons or Daughters, Husbands or Wives.

He's got you and it is God we must trust and follow.

He planned our future and all our tomorrow's

Memories

August 27, 2023

My memories are always there and they can be a comfort too
But the saddest memories are those made without you.
I remain grateful that I can still hear your voice and see your face
It makes me thankful for the life you lived and how you won your race
When I speak of how you lived I always seem to smile
I realize this is a blessing and I enjoy that for awhile
Some of the things I remember about you are your laughter and your style
It is hard to believe that I can love you more each day
When you went to Heaven I will still remember the pain of that day
God helps me when I'm feeling pretty low
He reminded me of your children and how they need to know
That your life and legacy will live on in our hearts and in our minds.
We welcome every memory of you being generous and kind.
To honor your memory was how the Foundation got its start
As we provide scholarships and help all children it also helps heal our broken heart.
We celebrate the love between a Mother and Son
And share God's love with everyone
We know you knew love and you gave love each day
It is hard without you so we ask God to guide our way
We grieve so much because we love so much is true
We have wonderful memories and thank God for the gift of you.
Till we meet up in Heaven our faith in the Lord will be our guide
We will gain our strength with the Lord by our side.
We are thankful for our memories of our time on Earth with you
We give God the glory for helping us in everything we do.

If All Roads Lead To You

June 3, 2023

If all roads lead to you Lord, then why do we take detours along the way?

And why do I find faults with others and act as tho I have no faults at all?

The only "PERFECT" one accepts everyone and waits for me to call.

Instead of me always finding faults with every one I see

I need to ask God to fix the faults in me.

Life has bends and turns and it's important to realize our blessings along the way

We need to be an encourager and be aware of the words we say.

If we truly care about others like Jesus has asked us to

Then we are following His example of what we should do.

We aren't here to judge and we certainly wouldn't want anyone to judge us

The Bible is a blueprint of where to place our trust.

All roads lead to you Lord, and our faith is in you

Help us erase detours from anything we choose to do.

Our time on Earth is short and we must help others to see

If we shift our focus and we will avoid the thought that the world revolves around me

Help us to be more in tune of others needs

We want you Lord to help us plant seeds

All roads need to lead straight to you

Then a deeper love for one another will be what we do.

Who's Looking At Me?

I look in the mirror and what do i see

I don't recognize who is looking at me

The stress and pain changed me no doubt

Losing a loved one is a pain that you don't want anyone to know about.

You let yourself go and do minimal chores

There is not a plan or a schedule in store.

It is a drastic change in health and looks

For this there is no self help book

Friends are well meaning but they tend to say the wrong thing

So depression deepens and isolation is what that brings.

Who's looking at me is The One who truly cares

He is constantly helping us when life seems too unfair.

We need to look at ourselves and know our worth.

God planned our life and has been with us since birth.

God doesn't make any mistakes and He will help us as we choose which road

Our God has plans for our future and for a happy life I'm told.

Who's looking at me

That is God and there is nothing He doesn't see

Trust in God's Promises and believe in Him, always.

God is who is looking at me and He has great plans for all of my days.

When the outside has faded and some wrinkles appear

Know that God knows your heart and He will make all things clear.

Who's looking at me?

It is God and He is smiling as He watches me release all fears to become free.

My Son Showed Me Jesus

December 23, 2023

My son showed me Jesus, his love sure did shine.

I am so happy that God knows this Son of mine.

He's gone to Heaven and now has his reward for the life he lived.

He sang about Jesus, and about the hope that only Jesus can give.

Jake is a walking testimony and an example of God's love.

And he praises our Father and the hope from above

My son showed me Jesus and praise God; others saw it too.

You knew of his love for Jesus in everything that he would say, and do.

I'm thankful for God, allowing me to be with my son for 34 years

And even though I know he is at peace, I still try to sort out my tears

My angel is in Heaven, will help calm any fear

They Didn't Make It

March 19, 2023

They didn't make it

Oh contrare

They did make it and they are happy there

We no longer can see or hear their voice

But they are with Jesus because of an earlier choice.

They accepted Jesus and always followed His ways

Forever knowing that eternal life comes

At the end of our earthly days.

They didn't make it, is often what is said

But depending on the life they led

They may be rejoicing with our Heavenly Father up above

And they have never felt more love!

We tend to cry and wish they could come back

But once they meet Jesus they won't want to even consider that

The joy of The Lord helps us to know

He has plans for us - the Bible tells us so.

This life is temporary and a better one awaits

We have a Heavenly Home inside those pearly gates.

Don't look at death as a final separation of our loved ones

Remember, that as a believer, they have truly won.

All of us will leave and we don't know what day

God waits for us to repent and follow His way

It is human nature to miss friends and family that we love

But God's Promises an eternal life in Heaven above.

Live your life and be mindful everyday

That it really matters what we do and what we say.

We aren't just here to take up space

We need to help others complete their race

We know not the number of our days

We should fill our hearts with words that the bible says

God gave it to us as a guide so we would know what to do

He wants all of us in Heaven and He is waiting on you

We just invite God into our hearts.

And the Holy Spirit will do His part.

We act as if nothing matters and tomorrow we can make it right

We live in darkness and argue, and fight

That truly is when they didn't make it - if they don't allow God to lead

It is no secret God's love is what we need.

Go about your day and thank God for the blessings you find

Every day make sure you are encouraging and kind

Then when God does call you home one day

They didn't make it - won't be what they say

Our Heavenly home is prepared and God wants no one to be left behind

Share his word daily and God's true peace you will always find.

I Try To Be Good

By doing what I should
We all know to do what's right
But sometimes we just lose sight
What we know to be true seems to fade
By justifying little exceptions that we made
It won't hurt if I do it just one time
That becomes a new habit of mine.
I try to be good and I take the right steps
Everything lines up but my secret excepts
It starts so innocent as habits often do
But all too often those habits consume you
I try to be good and God knows my heart
Why do I aim high and still miss my mark
Can I find my way and get on track
Or will it be one step forward and two step back
I try to be good and I know God will always love me
The devil wants me to feel desperate and too blind to see
That God's love is powerful and His promises are true
God wants us to repent and to know that He is for you.
I try to be good won't be what you continue to say
If you accept the life God has planned, you will know real joy everyday!

It's Not About Me And It's Not About You

July 7, 2015

It's not about me and it's not about you

We are supposed to show love in everything we do

We will all be judged one day

And have to give account for what we do and what we say

So please stop with your act and your judgemental way

Only God has that right on my final day

What I did or what I said

You can't seem to get out of your head.

When I'm in your presence our eyes never meet

And in your presence there's no conversation - you don't even speak!

It's okay, I'm learning how to forgive

And to use my time to really live!

God is who presence I long to be in

Not yours - you want only to point out my sin

You fail to recognize that you are at fault too

And judging me, doesn't speak well of you!

So try to remember it's not about me and it's not about you

And we ARE supposed to show love in everything we do!

Heavenly Home

I don't recognize my life these days

Some of the key people are missing and some friends have parted ways

I think that is what all of us experience sometime

We take love for granted and expect it to be fine

My Mom and Dad and our precious Son

Are out of sight and this is true

Our brothers and sisters too

They all have gone to Heaven - their race is won

We have been devastated and the loss of our Son.

These people you think will be with you for life and it is hard to let them go

They were so special and so fun to know

I trust in God to help me whenever I'm sad

It is so difficult at times to recall all the fun we had.

I believe that they are all walking on the streets of glory

It is awesome to share their life's story

Family is a blessing straight from above

Home is where we learn how to love

It always seems no matter how long they live

We can't imagine our lives without the family we want to be with

Friends are like family too

And tears are shed if they move away from you

There are lessons to learn from those that move away

Their time wass up and a season was all they were meant to stay.

You may not recognize your life these days

But we need to rely on God and follow His ways.

He has a place for us and the Bible says it is so

Trust in His word and let your faith grow

Let family and friends know how much you love them all the time

God may call them home and when He calls us we will find

That they are all happy in Heaven and they recognize your face

Our eternal life will begin when we have won our race.

Enjoy your time on Earth as you are passing thru

Heaven is real and your loved ones are waiting on you.

Oh My Word

April 10, 2022

Do you believe what you've heard?

Someone said it, so it must be true

Please, listen carefully, whatever you do.

You may never know how much your words weigh

To those on your path but they take note of what you say.

Whether we ever know our impact isn't the most important part

Our words can speak life and touch a heart.

On my word

It doesn't matter what you heard

Remember to respect that we are different and God made us that way

Build one another's confidence with the words you say.

Don't you know that you have power in your voice?

Being kind and loving is an easy choice.

Think about the joy you can share

By just using words that say you care

Let's say what we need to say

And remember to spread love each day

Never make judgements only God has that right

Let the power of your words be a shining light

Oh my word

With the love of God we can be free as a bird.

Find joy each and every day
Spend time with your loved ones
And don't delay
Our journey can be an interesting ride
Get busy living and travel far and wide!

My Son

August 28, 2017

I sit here tonight and think of my Son and what he chose to do
There are many people who would not do it, and that is surely true.
But he puts his trust in you God and in you alone
Even tho it's risky he has left his comfy home.

He knows a deeper trust and real value in this life
His trust is in you Lord and he will be back to his children and his wife.
How can he go and work so very far away
It is his faith in you Lord - he prays along the way!

It isn't a job that many would want to do
But I believe he counts it as pure joy - and he relies on you.
My Son has taught me so much, it should be the other way around.
I've learned a deeper love with you Lord, can be found.

I appreciate all the Angels that you have sent to be our guide
No task will be too hard - when God is on your side.
I sit here tonight and I think of my Son and it is all in a different light
With your guidance daily Lord, all things will work out just right!

Well No - You Didn't Have To Go

September 20, 2017

Well no,
You didn't have to go
And I wish you would have stayed with us till the end of time!
Because then I wouldn't have this huge broken heart of mine.

It broke the day you left us and went to your Heavenly home
That's great for you - but it leaves us hurting and feeling all alone.
Our God is with us too and now He has one more Heavenly aide.
To help look after us and remind us to praise all that God made!
Jake, you were a gift from day one
And watching you grow was so much fun!!
You always excelled in everything you did
Your love for our Lord was in constant view and was splendid!

Well, No,
You didn't have to go
But you did and Son, this is a fact
I can't wait to see your Heavenly home and be right where you're at!!
The life you lived in just a few years
Left a legacy of love and showed us not to fear
You have paved the way
And may I just say
You chose to stay on the high road
Forever Son, memories of you will always be told.

Well no,

You didn't have to go

And you being gone is the worst to accept.

I look to my memories and all the photos I've kept

I just loved the smile you flashed and your eyes shining so bright.

And I loved how you always took a stand for what is right!

Everyone knew that you and God walked hand in hand

You always let your light shine - you were just that kind of man!!

Well no,

You didn't have to go

But brave you stayed till the end.

You were the best Son, Husband, Father, Pastor and Friend!

We will find rest in the Lord and we know His promises are true

We love you Son and we will await to be reunited with you!!

Our Gifts From Above

December 25, 2018

From the time your child was first born
You were his everything.
But later in life, other relationships formed,
And he fell in love and gave her a ring.
Soon came the balance of leave him alone
And be there if he needed you.
You cherish each of his calls on the phone.
Then pray for more visits and calls to you.
You are busy building your life on earth too.
And as you stepped back to give them room;
Only God knew your child was going to his Heavenly home soon.
Then you are left with I wish I, and why didn't I?
You try to be strong but often break down and cry.
Be there for your loved ones and truly just be.
I'm sharing this now as it happened to me.
You back away and smile as your child grows to be a man.
Your heart fills with pride as you witness the beauty of God's plan.
Even though my outcome is different than what I would have thought.
I now see our Father's love,
and now understand more of what the Bible taught.
It's all in there and that's the key to help us learn how to live.
Such a beautiful gift, red letter words are a blessing; and our example of how to give.
Live each day and remember to express your love.
God directs our steps and He blesses us with our gifts from above.

Lord, I Ask You To Come Into My Heart

September 4, 2016

Lord, I ask you to come into my heart
I have no room for bitterness, unforgiving, or fear
I ask your help to mend relationships that have fallen apart
And rekindle the love of our family we hold so dear

There can be no true mending without you to guide
Please come into my heart and walk by my side
Help me to see the good in all I meet
Help me to desire to be your hands and feet

Be with me Lord as each day starts
Show me how to live a life that will honor you
Help me to apply your words in all I do

I love you Lord and on this Earth I sometimes feel so alone
But I long to praise your name till you call me home
Please give me words to help others to see
This hope of a brighter future you have placed in me!

Words Spoken

When I'm not talking - that helps me be free
I won't release all the anger that's built up inside of me!
I'll also be making sure my words don't offend
This saves relationships between family and friends

The tongue is sharper than a two edged sword, for real
Once words are spoken - they never return and that seals the deal
It's tough to conquer and combat the harm caused by a cruel remark
That's so hurtful and it breaks my heart

I've never required much in my life
And I pride myself on being a good Mom and a good Wife.
I know I fail and leave things undone
But it's never my intent to hurt anyone

I've been on both sides of hearing and saying words that are far from kind
That's different now - as I speak less of what comes to my mind
I count to ten, pause , pray and even take a walk
This makes a calmer and wiser choice when I talk

I only want peace and I'm trying to love all
That's another place where I stumble and fall
It's so easy to love most people we meet
But just being in the room with others spells defeat

It's a daily struggle to do the right thing
But Lord, help me to convey what I mean
Sometimes it's better to listen and try to hear you
And not just speak because you were spoken to

The words we say can wound or they can speak life
This is proven more difficult between husband and wife
We tend to nag and pick apart
All that ever does is chip at the heart

Lord, help does seem to be a daily request
He gave the example and wants me to do my best
This is the time to give others a lift and a smile
We have that chance with each text or number we dial.

When I'm not saying much - you can be sure of this
I want to hear your needs that I could fill - an opportunity not to miss.
I hope when you remember any conversations we've had -
You think of the good and there is no bad

The way we talk and the things we say
Will come back to us in some form or way
Speak kindly and try to use words that are sweet
And know it will help make friends of those that we meet

When we feel as though we are empty - we just need to look up

The Lord has a way to fill our cup

Never think that we walk alone

Our life can be a reflection of the love the Lord has shown!

Compare If You Dare

April 2, 2020

As you wake each day
Do you look in the mirror and say
Thank you Lord for this day you've given me
I will honor you and live and love freely
We need more appreciation for what you have formed
You knew me Lord before I was born
With you Lord, I see the world in a different light
Your plan is for our lives to shine bright

Compare if you dare
Contentment is rare
Why do we think others' lives are so fine?
When are we blessed and highly favored all the time.
God knows our struggles and all our victories too
There is never a time that God is not with you!
Don't try to fix or change the outcome of each day
Try to trust God more - He will always make a way.

Compare if you dare
Contentment is rare
Don't be the one that gets left alone
Invite Jesus in your heart and you will not go wrong
God knows the desires of our heart and HE can make all things new.
Let's walk with God and thank Him for the path that HE has chosen for you

Let's Hear It For The Songwriters

February 16, 2017

Let's hear it for the Songwriters
They make our lives brighter
They say what we mean, when we don't mean what we say
Can we get more Songwriters today!

Some songs are taken for granted
Yet they bloom in our hearts and minds once they're planted
A Songwriters tools are words, simply words
With an awesome power - once heard

Although a Songwriters tools are mere words in various formats,
They become a constant reminder of where we've been - or to where we are at!
A light at the end of the tunnel can be easier to see -
When a song describes my life so perfectly

Ah, the Songwriter can build a bridge or mend some fences;
By combining the right music to words in sentences!!
You can count on them to tell it like it is
Without much thought of making it into Show-Biz
Their only thought is to try to relate
A thing, a person, or a special date

You know words, simply words, are a part of each day
But there is a result from the things we say
It's ok we all need help with our words now and then
And someone will know too well where we've been

It's a natural release for a talented few,
To add music and lyrics and compose songs, just for you
When out of context somethings can be taken wrong
A Songwriter can soothe us, by saying it in a song!

Each masterpiece is written with life's journeys in mind,
Along some roads that are not always kind.
It is said a pen can be mightier than a sword
When thoughts - onto paper - are poured
Real talent is in the correct combination of right words, music, and timing
For the complete package is much more than just rhyming

A Songwriter is an instrument which can bring words to life
Words that tell of happiness, love or strife
Each struggle or period which we have endured at any time
We managed to get thru it and come out fine
Each day when a song is heard -
We are taken back to one moment, or one word.
Yes a Songwriters words work magic - it's true
A memory preserved - for me - and you!!!

Willie Bound

March 25, 2007

Willie bound, Willie bound
Happens easily whenever he's in town
We watch him charm the crowd with a song
Which tells stories of times and things that went wrong
It's exciting to see how Willie tells of everyday things
That seems clearer with the words he sings.

The guitar he plays is amazing to hear
And his unique style of playing - so pleasing to the ear

A deeper respect for him has developed more as each year passes
For this songwriter/musician remains tops in both classes
We know he can play and sing a song
But the list of Willie accomplishments is very long
Farm-aid and biodiesel to name only two
There is still much more for Willie to do!!
So put on his music and let his words inspire
Each of us to value others more, and help lift them up higher!!

The age thing doesn't seem to slow Willie down
So make sure you are there next time he's in town!!

Mick And Me

April 8, 2019

Let me tell you about Mick and me

We are having the same surgery but maybe done differently

God gave us everything - this is true

So knowing it's His plan - trust is what we do

The lucky day was when our heart problem was found

The angel in our heart - will help us to stay around!

Then you can have sympathy for the devil because he did not win

Our recovery wasn't in his plan - but we will shine a light again

Wild horses are carrying our wandering spirit still

Our charmed life will reflect God's will

Old habits die hard and we will study on that a bit more

We will be dancing in the streets or whatever God has in store

When the devil tried to do us in and put us in the trash can

God intervened and reminded us that He has the best plan!

You can't always get what you want - that maybe right

But with God our surgery was just another night.

Joy comes in the morning for real

God rescued us and with Him we will heal

Get a grip people, and live right each day

We are lucky in love and our God paves our way!

Mick and me went thru the same type of surgery, this is true

But we came out convinced that God is the right choice for me and you!!

The Change We Need Begins With You!

April 20, 2017

Each day we can make the difference we want to see
One kind word or smile might just set someone free!
What a joy to know that simple gesture could change someone's heart
Be that change - by being good and doing your part

Not That Different

We are different you and I
That doesn't mean that I don't try
I understand a carefree style gives you peace
But I'm talking with God more and learning to release
To really love a person you should accept them, flaws and all
I know that judging them is not my call
God knows our heart and our intent
We need to gain focus and let our time be better spent.
We don't have time to waste on being full of regret
So let's remember who holds our future and who makes sure our needs are met
God knows we are human and He forgives when we sin
God's word we can stand and trust that we win.
Although we may be different you and I
We have the same reference to live by
Give the Bible a good read
It has the answers and it plants the seed.
Together we see growth in our minds as they are daily fed
The bible has red letters to remind us of what God said
When we are united we stand on God's word
What's seen with the eye is better than what's heard
Things repeated can get twisted and thus taken the wrong way
It's best to read God's word for yourself each day
Our lives can be much different, I believe this is true
If we let it be our goal to honor God in all we do
There are people we can reach and we can make sure they know

About the promises of God as we share scripture in their lives we will sow

We reap the harvest and welcome all in

Our differences are forgotten now our united goal is to win

Face Life

Instead of just looking at Facebook each day

Be more aware of what you like and what you say.

We are called to face life

Any words harshly spoken can cut like a knife

Hurting people, hurt people, and this cycle can go on and on.

Our need to win is just to be able to say that we won

When we face life, we learn to see joy in others wins and to say well done

Forgiveness can be hard and we need time for some wounds to heal.

We are called to "face life" and to figure out how to deal

Our struggles that seem too hard to do

Become less stressful if we remain positive and thankful too

Facebook is a tool that helps us keep up with our family and friends

Face Life by embracing each day by giving love without end.

God Is The Current

As we go through our lives each day
Do we ever thank God or stop to pray?
God is in the current current, in the river of life
With HIS help our relationships have less strife.
Loved ones who really matter are often our last thought
We take for granted this love that can't be bought.
God is in the current meet Him and go with the flow
God can do all things and He will be with you wherever you go.
When life's waters move too swiftly and we get tossed to and fro
We pray to God asking for the answers we need to know
We all seek a love that is unconditional and true.
That is exactly what God has for you
God is in the current and He will point the way
We just give Him our heart and repent and pray.
We pray for others as they need God's love too.
Always thank God for the work He has done in you
God is in the current and He wants to be with us each day
Relax and Trust God
He will always find a way

Sands Of Time

As we go about our day today

Let's focus less on what others say

Finding fault comes easy so rise above that train of thought and see

If you and I can work together - we will find the value of living stress free

Our days may seem like they are going by faster

Be mindful of our goal to be with Our Master

The gift of life is comes with a blank slate

We fill in those gaps by the choices we make

Our days are truly like the sands of time, so spend them wisely and make sure others do
too

Kindness goes a long way and it says volumes about you!

Have no regrets and finish what you start.

It's important to find our way and to do our part.

Our blessings are some ways that God showers His love on us

Let God's light be the beacon of hope and trust.

Every minute that is wasted can never return

What Level Of Sin

What level of sin are you knee deep in? Is it obvious or do you hide?

The angels know you've tried

To act like you are problem free

But that meanole mirror just won't let you be!

It doen't sugar coat any side affect of any current abuse

Instead it reminds you - you're on a short fuse!

To justify and deny and then get caught

So was it worth the good time that it bought?

We all find ways to escape every now and then

But is your choice any type of sin?

There are no levels of sin, one is just as bad as the other

For a sin can be not honoring your father and mother

Or as bad as hating your brother

How about if you plan to steal

They are all sins - and the end result is real!

Yes, we sit back and say 'but I didn't kill"

But did you lie, cheat, or have your hand in the till?

Never try to be in the seat like a judge

But know that we need to forgive or drop a grudge

Our habits can be so old that we just accept

Or we live with a fear and constant reject

Whether it's made up - or if indeed a fact
We are either accepted and welcomed in a pack
Or we isolate ourselves and feel down in the dumps
People get excluded or they exclude themselves and make a mountain out of a hump!
So many things and items can affect our health
We see that it's much more important than wealth.

It is true that divorce is a sin too
You can't always tell if they really love you!
So you see many ways we can compare
Or see faults in others that you may share

The true testimony you've been given
Is the way it impacts the life you're living!
Anything in excess can become a sin
Don't worry about the levels - just give in!

The higher power that reigns over the universe
Is the way of happiness - and of removing your curse
No level of sin should ever let you forget
We all will answer to one judge - and we've not met Him yet!

Don't stare at those who aren't just like you
Love them, accept them, and go do what you can do
Others are hurting and desire a way out
Instead of your silence, tell them what Heaven is about.

A desire to change and a willing heart
No other way will you have a new start
Forget about any level of sin
And allow the Heavenly Father to live within!

No amount of food, shopping, pill, or alcohol will ever be enough to fill
The empty life when we are out of "God's Will"
For His desire and plan for us is well defined
Surrender, follow Jesus and our lives are back in line

We will be following His example we love all we see
And then the level of sin you're knee deep in will fade away and set you free!

Peace With Jesus

My eyesight is fading but I see you perfectly clear

The love I have for Jesus has become deeper and oh, so dear

I feel far more than I can say

God has blessed me in so many ways

I'm not where I need to be

But my prayer is that you see the Jesus in me

Be thankful and know that Jesus is for you

Don't forget to acknowledge Jesus in all that you do

Remain thankful and let Jesus guide

What you say to be honest and true

Read his word and let His love be a light that reveals peace to make all things new

God Gave Us Eyes To See

May 20, 2022

God gave us eyes to see

But we look at things different you and me

Some people buy a RV to travel the world so wide

Others are more content just staying inside

We know that God gave us eyes to see

This gift proves how different we can be

One sees the sky and imagines Heaven above

When another spews hate and doesn't know love

God gave us eyes to see

He sends His Angels for you and for me!

Call on God and believe His word is true

Ask Him into your heart and He will make all things new.

When you look and make the effort to see

You will be more certain of God's love for you and for me

We need to help others to see the light

Share your testimony and how you got your heart right

Our job is to just plant the seed

As we find our path in life, we help those in need

God provides our seed to sow

He provides our friends who help if we are feeling low.

Our eyesight is a blessing that is so true

God gave us eyes to see and He wants the best for me and for you

Look for ways to help others if you can

Each day things happen and they are part of God's plan

God gave us eyes to see

Repent and forgive if need be.
You were the prisoner that needed set free.
Thank you God for giving us eyes to see.

The Great Train Ride

October 23, 2025

They are planning a special family time

Richard, Pat, Vicky and Jerry are ready to rise and shine

In just a few days

They'll be on their way

Leaving Sulphur Springs headed to Union station to connect with Amtrak for the great train ride

Anticipation builds, they are fit to be tied

When we age trips are few and far between,

So this little piece of Heaven will provide BEAUTY they've never seen

They're heading to Oklahoma to see all of the sites

All through the day and up into the night

So much to do, so much to see

Taken into the beautiful sights like the colors of the trees

We all have the opportunity to see the beauty God has made

Sometimes the beauty is a bench placed perfectly in the shade

That will allow a short break and a chance to rest

For you want to be alert and at your best

When you hear about trips and the detail that they are planned

You envision happiness and couples walking hand in hand

The great train ride it's how this is billed

A chance to slow down and allow our minds to be healed

Some of us don't need to go and probably are fine with that fact

But those who continue to plan and appreciate life are a real class act

Horse races, sightseeing, and so many memories will be formed

Just because the adventurous spirit seeks to leave behind the norm

The great train ride will be a spectacular treat
God will provide the beauty and the kind folks for you to meet
Have fun my friends and enjoy your train ride
Richard, Pat and Vicky, with Jerry by her side
This is exciting even as I hear your plans
My sweet friends, love of life and still holding hands!

Can You See Me

April 9, 2022

Can you see me?
Help me if I am confused.
Things are changing and I can't keep up
Mine is not half full or empty, I can't even find my cup.
When you look at situations and your health is good
You handle business and communicate when you should.
Then as if a switch is turned off things are not the same
You look like you did and you have the same name.
But silently the biggest change is in your mind.
It might start as being anxious and scared to unwind.
Then it is more apparent the changes are real
Others can now see and even understand how you feel
Slipping away and losing ability to communicate is the reality and a sad fact for sure
The worst part is there is no cure.

Can you see me?
Don't take for granted what you see
As we go thru life we know that many changes will be made
Often they go unnoticed until our memory starts to fade.
Heaven only knows why some families escape what others must endure
This gradual mental decline becomes childlike and pure
Watching this happen is hard to understand
Its effects alter with no mercy on women or men.
Can you see me?
Let's visit and be thankful we are free

The person you see wants to remember and longs for your touch
If you will take time you can connect with the one you love so much.
Can you see me?
Help me, love me, and help me be...

Tragedy

When tragedy comes, our immediate thought is to gather the troops but in reality we tend to isolate and retreat to help process.

We always think our loved ones will be there forever and so we take our friends and family for granted.

At times we think tomorrow we will make it right. Tomorrow doesn't come for everyone and we must be more aware of that today.

We often say "he was one of the good ones" but there is good in each of us, and it is up to us to add to the good within us, and be the best we can be.

We get better when we try, and the days we are weak we can call on The Lord to hold us when we cry.

Trust in Him and His plans. God is with us and He holds our future in His hands.

Tragedy does come and we don't know when or why...

God wants us to help others live and to not be afraid to die.

We have the promise of eternity to spend in Heaven above.

Thankful for the comfort and peace that comes with His unending love

Help others to remember to thank God for helping you

God's Promises are eternal and He will never stop loving you.

The Revival

February 17, 2007

I went to a revival the other night
When an Evangelist from Oklahoma talked about getting right
For once, I was listening and it sank in...
And I want to Thank You, Thank you, Thank You for this joy in my heart.
Yes, Thanks to you Jesus; I have a fresh start!
I'll confess my sins and share your story -
That's my new path... now I'm headed to glory.

That night the miracles of our Lord were told in song;
We kept praising our Savior; and the service was long!
The LoveJoy Singers lifted their voices in song - too -
And they sang about "Mama, Praying For You"
The Holy Spirit blessed us and the Church we were in
Thanks be to God for the forgiveness of Sin.

Well if you're ever invited to a revival... please go
Traveling Preachers can be a pleasure to know.
Their mission is to bring God's Love into our home
And tell the best news; we are not alone!!!
It's great to see the love a complete stranger can bring
When they come Worship, Teach, or Sing.
We are reminded that God is powerful and His blessings are all around
And how an Everlasting Life IN CHRIST - can be found.

As the Services were closing in prayer;

It stirred a friend who was there

To tell an awesome testimony - she was meant to share.

For just 6 months ago the Doctors didn't know

How a couple could survive after being tossed around so

There was a point that the outlook was grim

That was before the area Churches came in

The Testimony that she gave was all in God's Plan...

For all the Church Members had helped to "Pray her Well"

And on this night she was there to shake their hands.

Surviving a Near-Fatal Motorcycle Accident - Her miracle to tell!!

What a Blessing when a Church really cares

And are shown the rewards of uniting in prayer.

Our lives can be forever changed;

Health restored, Love Rekindled, no story is the same.

The Lord is most gracious and always knows just what we need;

He places people in our lives so they can plant the seed

Oh what a blessing when our Lives are made new

When our Sins are Forgiven and Forgotten too!

Mom's Teaching

December 13, 2016

She taught us how to live each day
By encouraging us to watch what we say
For unkind words can break a heart
So be mindful of their impact before you start!

She taught us love and spoke of scripture without the Bible in tow
Her teachings are etched in my memory, I love her so!
Cherish your parents and please listen to the good
They want the best for you so give love as a child should.

The prayers of our fathers and mothers are passed down
And in those sweet acts of love is where God is found
Practice doing good as our parents taught us to each day
And pass down their lifetime of love and teaching in all that we say!

Mom

October 17, 2009

As I sit here and watch you sleep
The radio is playing "Cry out to Jesus", I have a pen in hand
I'm overcome with sadness and begin to weep
For I realize your body is quitting, it has done all it can.

Once again, you have fought a great fight
But the sickness is winning, maybe tonight.
Mom, no one can hold a candle to you
Reasons are too numerous and there's no one can do all you do!

The family has always had the pleasure of your rallying in every case
But this illness is winning with haste
I really wish I could take away your pain
And have you healthy, happy, strolling down memory lane

Reminiscing has been fun with you, always!
For you remembered details of the good ole days
Like when you and John put a cat on the hot stove and got caught
That's when a hard whipping and serious lesson was taught
The cat was quick to learn

One paw in the fire, and you get burned
No humor was found in this act by your Mother
But this story got more giggles than any other.

Simple homemade fun, that's what you were best at
Even if it burned a few toes of an unexpecting cat
That is the only thing I've ever known you to harm
As you grew up with the simple life on the farm.

Mom, I cherish the life you and Dad created for me
And I apologize for not appreciating and acknowledging what I now can see
All you ever wanted was love and happiness from us kids
So sorry, we failed you and many of us kept our love hid.

Now when you need us, we are by your side
Aching so much and wanting you well and knowing the doctors have tried
Heaven awaits the perfect Angel Mom I know you are
You will light up the sky as you are the brightest star

Mom's Home

August 27, 2009

The news came today, and some would say that it is bad.
For when a loved one hurts, well, that is sad
But according to doctors, who are trained to know,
Her condition is deteriorating and her strength is low.

She is scheduled to come home tomorrow and we will be at her side,
To support, get supplies, and help in any way
Or just be there to listen to what she might say.
You realize too late, that she means the whole world
Time is precious, and it is slipping away.
Why didn't I call her yesterday?

Or why didn't I go and hold her hand,
Why now am I worrying about the grains of sand
For when my mom does leave this earth,
She'll have a new body, new name, new birth.
God will wrap her in his loving arms.
He alone can shelter her from any more harm!

Of course the children look forward to mom coming home,
Even tho she sits in her wheelchair, all alone.
For most of her days are spent just that way,
Unless someone takes time to stop by and say
Well, anything at all, or maybe read God's word.
That would lift her spirits and she would remember what she heard!

It is strange how someone who means so much get taken for granted and that,
We will never know how it felt unless we sat where she sat!
Cause when we would listen as others made their plans to go and to do
And then remember their plans don't include you.

For "it might be too much trouble" mom could hear them say
'She can't walk and might get in the way'.
Well, go on and make the plans that were so important to you,
For now mom's busy and she's got much to do!

She's focused on things that we can't understand
God's leading her and He is holding her hand!
Mom's home and what joy and peace at last!
No pain or sorrow and all her fears have been cast
Far to the east and to the west never again to take a hold.
Mom's life has been a testimony of God's love
A treasure worth more than gold!

Many years while walking this earth,
She sang to her children, starting at birth.
She sang of Christ's love and how He died for us.
She'd tell us those stories and she'd tell us not to cuss!

Oh mom, how special you are and you alone
And I welcome the day that God calls me home!
Till then I will remember all those stories and I'll pray each day
That God will reign in my life, and make a way.

I love you mom, and my life you always bless
Come home mom and find some rest.

Mother Dear

October 17, 2009

Mother Dear, Mother Dear
Her sweet voice echoes in my ear.
She's the one to count on each day
To sing our praises, and have something nice to say!

Although some times may have been hard,
On your special occasion, she'd send a card.
Quite often, she would include a small note,
Oh how I cherish the lines that she wrote.

Mom loved children and she had eight,
3 boys, 5 girls, meant daily debates
Mom would do roll call till she got to your name,
She always knew what child was to blame.

As we age comes a new appreciation for those good old days,
Like when Mom made us wax windowsills when company came.
And she even made waxing the floors a game.
Sometimes Dad brought home a floor waxer,
Other times Mom pulled us in sheets, floors shined much faster!

The things you experience, the love you are shown,
All acknowledged more when you are full grown
A child would not realize how precious Mother Dear really can be,
It's thru aging alone that we can see

That all Mother Dear ever wanted from us
Is for us to be happy and that we not fuss.

She's aging now and so are we
And her strong values are very clear to me
Love, listen, laugh and learn with your Mother Dear today
Show her respect and that you're thankful in many ways!!
Make her smile and brighten up her days.
Mother Dear, we may never know,
How one person could express her love so.

It is our turn now to just love you and help in any way we can,
To give you our support, our heart, and our hand
You are the reason for this life we are living
Thanks for the peace and all the love you have given.

Mother Dear, it is forever a prayer in my heart
That all of your days have a great start
And that God will work thru you as he has always done
When he helped you raise 5 daughters and 3 sons!!
Your devotion and pure love given freely to this family
Mother Dear, a lifetime friend to me!

Now when you need us, we are by your side,
Aching so much and wanting you well.
And knowing the doctors have tried.
Heaven awaits the perfect angel mom I know you are.
You will light up the sky as you are the brightest star!

My Dad

January 12, 2016

I remember the day my Dad died.
Oh, I remember how we cried.
Dad was so tough, how could it be,
That a car accident could take him from me!

Our lives were shattered on that cold night
And even today it doesn't seem right.
Dad was a man of few words,
But when he spoke his message was heard.

God, how I loved my Dad and what a huge loss for all
Everything changed when I got Mom's call!!
She didn't drive and she had to wait to find out his fate
I called the hospital and was told that it was too late.

Gone in an instant was such a great man, my Dad
Gone was the strongest love my Mom ever had!
It has been years and tears still flow
Amazing that with time I still hurt so.

Dad deserves every tear I've shed
For he was a true hero in the life he led.
Dad went to the Army and was a highly decorated Vet
He got a Purple Heart, made it home cause God wasn't done with him yet.

How proud of my Dad I will always be
And in my heart I know he was proud of me.
Cherish your Dad if you are blessed to have one still living,
Talk to him, hug him, and be aware of all he is giving.

In a second all that's good can be taken from you.
Make sure the love you are given is given back too!
Don't wait to say what you wish you would have to your loved one
Everyday be the best Daughter or Son.

Angel Debbie

She was the smartest of us girls

And the prettiest in all the world.

She never hurt anyone

And she was always a lot of fun.

I've always looked up to her as my big sis

And her beautiful smile will surely be missed

I can remember trying one of her shirts

That made me feel pretty, and less like a nerd.

I love Debbie and my heart is hurting so

God now has the angel, many got to know

She was always good to talk to

She listened and seemed to really care about you.

I pray that if you have a big sis like mine,

You'll call or write and go spend some time.

In a moment life can change and never be the same,

Care about your family, not just fortune and fame.

Our family is God's blessing for us to love.

So love your parents and siblings, they are true gifts from above.

Thankful today for Debbie such a warm sight

Lord be with us as we try to be alright

She suffers no more and in your arms will rest

For God has our angel, because He only takes the best.

DEBORAH RAYE (EPPERSON) HENKEL
July 24, 1950 – October 24, 2015

"This One"

July 24, 2018

He was not a me too person, no, he stood alone

He found Jesus and a much deeper love that he had ever known.

Jake would be right there for you, that was just his way.

He kept the faith, soared with the Eagles, and then followed as the Angels led that day.

"This One" is pretty special, let's look at the life he led.

With much joy they told stories of all the souls he fed.

Angels welcomed him with open arms and they took note of his winning smile.

They were amazed how this man's love stretched across so many miles,

"This One" was greatly loved from the very start.

He touched many lives and melted many hearts.

He was kind and caring and very brave and strong.

His time on earth was short, some did not know him long.

"This one" just had a way to spread God's love.

He shared God's word and he sang praises to our Lord above.

It is a blessing to witness the word alive and see it shining bright in a mortal man.

Jake is now in paradise - "This One" is in the Promised Land.

JAKE CHARLES WILSON
July 12, 1983 – August 30, 2017

When I'm Gone

When I come to the end of my journey
And I travel my last weary mile
Just forget if you can, that I ever frowned
And just remember only the smile.

Forget unkind words I have spoken,
Remember some good I have done.
Forget that I ever had heartache,
And remember I've had loads of fun.

Forget that I've stumbled and blundered,
And sometimes fell by the way.
Remember i have fought some hard battles,
And won, by the close of the day.

Then forget to grieve for my going,
I would not have you sad for a day.
But in the summer just gather some flowers,
And remember the place where I lay.

That's Not My Norm

We have become numb
To horrible news, reports about somebody acting dumb
They leave beautiful babies in unsafe places
This is a fact, and it's being done by all races!

Too often you hear about children strapped in their car seat
Great idea, but not be left alone to die in the heat!
These reports are so frequent, I shutter to think
How much lower can people really sink?

As I watched the news tonight
I could not believe how many people just aren't thinking right!
They have no thought about consequence of their choices,
They are fueled by hatred and they are using their voices.

And then as you might have already guessed
They end up harming others and making a mess!
Some messes can't be cleaned up or swept under a rug,
Poor choices today of using our arms to hold weapons instead of to give hugs

Yes hearing stories like this we tend to be numb
As they are just more reminders of people being dumb!
They pick on the young or the older folks that are frail
Too frequently do we hear an unimaginable tale.

There is some parent that doesn't want their bundle of joy,
They wanted a girl but they got a boy.
The excuses for poor judgement are numerous for sure
There is one thing that will be the cure

To end the hatred and disregard of our mere existence on earth
Kindness needs to be taught and practiced starting at birth!
Love for each other needs to always be shown,
So that we can be responsible adults when we are grown.

Kindness matters and it's much more than what we say
If we could be more considerate of others each day.
Hatred has no place in our hearts to form
I don't want to let this become my norm.

Don't become immune to the horrible news
It is always someone depressed and not having a clue!
They get high on hatred or alcohol or drugs
And they act out about what they don't like or what has them bugged.

And to think a moments rage
Would for some re-write their life's page
We can't have a do over if our violent behaviour lands us in jail
Hope would come from simply repenting when we fail.

So don't hear horrible news and say I wish there was something I could do,
We should know that the answer is inside of you.
Pray for the offender and victim and ask God to help
Choices are made and we place blame on ourselves!

That's not my norm to turn a blind eye,
Let's lift one another and don't pass them by!

I Ain't Got No Use For Abuse

May 27, 2017

I ain't got no use for abuse in any form.
If it is done once, soon it will be the"norm".
There are different forms of abuse, this is so true!
My prayer is that it never happens to you!

Abuse in the home, workplace, school, and all areas in between,
There is no excuse for it, and it is downright mean!
I have no magic wand or I would wave it,
And then perhaps a child's innocence - I could have saved it!

Young and old can be an easy target for sure
At any time some demon will try to lure.
And if we fall into their dirty trap,
They will harm us mentally and physically with all their crap!!

I have no use for abuse, and I just want to say
If any way you have been this person, stop it today!
Our homes should be a place where we are comfortable and we have peace
So, if your home is not peaceful, then let the madness cease!

There are no take backs on hits or on ugly words
And no eraser for a child to un-hear what they've heard.
I truly beg you to stop and look at your private times,
Make sure to have concern for others, and be ever mindful - abuse is a crime!

We should never have to report a loved one for an altercation or a dirty deed
But that should happen if someone is abused, or in need!
God be with us and allow our eyes to see,
We are created for love and kindness and the change begins with me!

I Apologize

March 19, 2009

Please let me apologize first to you, Lord.

Then to my husband and family and friends.

My list of people I've wronged never ends!

But Lord, my biggest failure has been to you.

For a good servant - I've never been, even tho I know I should

And I've lost count of all the times I had opportunity and saw plenty to do.

But I was selfish and said I'd help next time - "if I could"

Lord, please forgive me and give to me a servants heart

As of today, I'd love a brand new start

To show you I love you, and do my best to spread your word

To all I encounter and to always inquire if they've heard

The world's greatest story that has ever been told

A story more precious than diamonds or gold

The story of Jesus and the life he has planned

For every woman, child, and man.

In my apologies here I must include

For to my brothers and sisters, I have been rude.

Many accept my selfish ways

And say they'll love me all my days

But Lord I know i've missed the mark

When I know some that still walk in the dark

For you have said, you are the truth, the way, and the light

How can I forgive myself if I don't tell them what's right?

In your word, all answers are given

For a life that's rich and so worth living.

Please Lord, forgive me and accept my deep apology today
For not putting you first and being of service, for no pay!
For your plans are the best tip a server could ask for
Our mansion awaits at Heaven's door!
You're the one who knows our days on this earth
You know all things that will happen to us even before birth.
I pray, Lord, that with my time I have left here
I will make my love for you perfectly clear
Not only by the things I say
But by my actions each and every day!
Thank you for all you have given to me
And please, Lord, continue with your mighty work in me!

Second Guessing

November 25, 2009

Second guessing, that's what I always do
Wondering if what is said would somehow hurt you!
Second guessing, and thinking of yesterday
Did you really understand and listen to what I had to say
Or did my words fall on closed ears
And will I never let go of these fears
That somehow when I truly give from the heart
It backfires, derails, and that's not the worst part
Second guessing will destroy your self-esteem
Make good on your word and be sure to say what you mean!
Second guessing will tug at your heart,
You question all situations right from the start
They say "what don't kill you, will make you strong"
And then the one about "righting a wrong".
The point to get is simply the true fact,
Decide how you can proceed each day with grace and tact!
We make our own choices and the results aren't always good
But a lesson can be learned, if before we react, we would
Remember there are people in need
And we are supposed to be planting a seed
Second guessing, no longer will be a necessary thing to do
Being strong, speaking with love, that's what I always knew!
No guess work, that was what God intended
Show compassion and love and life will be splendid!
As we go about our everyday tasks,

There are memories made and feelings that last

Others may judge you and pick you apart

So your words and actions should come from your heart!

There will be times when doubt will still be there

When truths and love is what we share

The right thing to do is to speak with love

And be ever mindful of our Father above!

He created us and wants the best for us each day

His love, should be conveyed in all that we say!

What our "intent" was will always be defined,

When we carefully word those thoughts in our mind.

And sometimes It's abundantly clear that we struck the right note

When we receive a smile about what we said or wrote!

Second guessing, that's not in my plans,

As with all things, it's in God's hands!

For this is a time that I have been given

To show others peace and happiness and get on with living!!

Second guessing, comes from an anxious mind,

Stand on God's word, truths, leave your worries behind!

Second guessing, that's no longer for me,

Starting today, I'll be the sure person I was meant to be!

Get Busy Living And Loving

December 14, 2016

My sis sent a text today that said her friend Jan's sister had passed
She had cancer and was given two month, but didn't last
My sister said that she couldn't breathe and was unable to speak
The cancer took over and left her body too weak

We can all learn from this family's pain and sorrow
And have the realization that we aren't promised tomorrow.
We choose to be mad and leave our family or a friend to wonder why
I guess we think we will make amends before we die.

The main point I wish to get across
Is we never know what we had till it is lost
Give a friend, a loved one, or even a stranger a hug today
Speak kindly, they may hang on each word you say
I thought of my sister, and her friend's family's pain of their loss
And decided to "be there" for others more, no matter the cost.

It is really a small price to have lost some sleep
If we are talking with our friend and weeping when they weep
We tend to run thru most of this thing called life.
And spend our days working, tolling and have much strife.

It's not till the end of our time that we focus on someone else's pain
We have 24 hours each day, and we can let Heaven be our gain!

Lift up a love one and please pray
God knows your heart and hears each word you say
We might not be able to add another minute or another day
But we can comfort others that God sends our way.

Christmas Ain't Jolly Without Holly

June 14, 2017

She came into my life and a big change began.
It was as tho God smiled on the old man
We fell in love and all on this Earth was great,
And we were inseparable from our first date!

But things got rocky and she treated me more like a friend
How did such a beautiful love come to an end?
I really thought she was the one for me
Those memories we made were only special to me.

Christmas became our favorite time of year
A time meant to express love for all we hold dear
And to think that this was my true love, my dolly
Well now, Christmas ain't jolly without Holly!

Each Christmas, I'll remember the time we had
And all the good memories, I'll forget the bad!
Christmas ain't jolly without Holly, and that's true
But God always has plans for you
The joy will really be with us each day
If we give thanks and remember to pray!!

And so now I know that it wasn't in God's plan

For Holly to stay with this old man.

Even tho each Christmas ain't jolly without Holly with me,

Christmas remains God's perfect story, now I see

That God will always let His light shine

And the Christmas memories will always be mine!

Christmas Time

June 14, 2007

I remember Christmas and how it used to be
With the presents stalked underneath the tree
Bah Humbug never entered our mind
Friends and family were always kind

We'd help mom cook pumpkin pie
And watch movies of days gone by
In one my uncle was in a Santa suit
In another was my Dad wearing snow boots.

Even tho times were hard, we never suffered
If anything, we all just got tougher!
Though times don't last, but though people do,
And Christmas memories always bring joy to you

So hang the mistletoe and find a star for your tree
And you'll be remembering a Christmas like me
Christmas Time, Christmas Time
Memories forever planted in my mind
A time from long ago
Can always warm my heart so.

Christmas In Our Heart

June 14, 2007

Christmas in our heart
Tells of our new start
God is gracious and His blessings flow
Christmas in our heart
Comes from the Saviour we know!

Although many a day has gone by since Christmas was here
The joy and magic of this special time will stay with us forever.
The songs and the laughter when friends and family are near
The good food prepared by ones so clever.

We all know that God is love
And that our daily blessings come from above
This precious love and our gifts are meant to be shared
Our blessings came, because He cared.

So with God's grace we've been given time on this Earth
A learning process begins right from birth
The Kingdom awaits for those who put God first all the time
This is simple truth that needs to be spoken
A reminder of all the commandments, not to be broken
Just share God's words daily and all will be fine.

Christmas in our heart

Tell of our new start

God is gracious and His blessings flow

Christmas in our heart

Comes from the Savior we know!

THE JAKE C. WILSON MEMORIAL FOUNDATION, INC.

Celebrating the love between a mother and son and sharing God's love with everyone.

In his short 34 years, Jake Wilson touched many lives, serving as a children's pastor, praise and worship leader and working in prison ministry.

He loved the Lord and cherished his five children with all his heart. He also had a passion for fishing, hunting and singing and was well respected by his peers in the gas pipeline industry, where he made many friends he considered family.

He approached everything he did with kindness, warmth and an openness that spread itself easily among others.

The Jake C. Wilson Memorial Foundation, Inc, was created in 2018 to honor Jake's life and legacy. Jake's zest for life was contagious, and it's in this spirit that the Foundation has grown and developed many ways to help children.

Since its inception, the Foundation has:

- Helped create scholarships for children to attend Christian summer camps.
- Helped provide equipment for area high school fishing teams.
- Developed a scholarship at Jake's alma mater, Terrell High School.
- Established an annual team fishing tournament at Lake Fork.
- Provided other scholarship opportunities for students.

Our goal is to provide educational resources to children and to provide opportunities that will enrich their lives.

HOW CAN I HELP?

So glad you asked. Donations are always welcome and appreciated, or you might consider becoming a sponsor in the Jake C. Wilson Memorial Foundation, Inc. Annual Team Fishing Tournament.

This one-day team bass fishing event, held on world-famous Lake Fork, has grown each year since our first in 2018. The funds we raise are distributed to selected children's organizations that advance education and social group participation.

Sponsorship levels are available from $500 to $5,000.

To find out more about The Jake C. Wilson Memorial Foundation, Inc. or the bass tournament, please contact us or visit us on the web.

940-208-JAKE (5253)
www.jakecwilson.com
info@jakecwilson.com

Jake C. Wilson Memorial Foundation, Inc. is a 501(c)3 non-profit organization

About The Author

Diane Wilson

Diane Wilson was born in Muskogee, Oklahoma and grew up with deep Texas roots. She has spent her life writing down her thoughts, prayers, and the dreams she holds for a kinder world. Poetry became her way of working through joy, sorrow, and the seasons that shaped her, especially after the loss of her only son Jake in 2017 and her husband Charley in 2025.

Her hope is that these poems will comfort, inspire, and remind readers that God is near in every moment. Diane believes words carry power, and her Texas heart is always reaching to encourage others and lift their spirits.

Thank you for holding her story in your hands. May Straight From My Heart touch your life the way writing it touched hers.